# FOUND:
## GOD'S WILL

# FOUND:
## GOD'S WILL

FIND THE DIRECTION AND
PURPOSE GOD WANTS
FOR YOUR LIFE

## JOHN MACARTHUR

transforming lives together

FOUND: GOD'S WILL
Published by David C Cook
4050 Lee Vance Drive
Colorado Springs, CO 80918 U.S.A.

David C Cook U.K., Kingsway Communications
Eastbourne, East Sussex BN23 6NT, England

The graphic circle C logo is a registered
trademark of David C Cook.

LCCN 2012934188
ISBN 978-1-4347-0298-2
eISBN 978-0-7814-0360-3

The Team: Alex Field, Amy Konyndyk,
Jack Campbell, Karen Athen
Cover Design: Nick Lee
Cover Photo: Shutterstock

Printed in the United States of America
Third Edition 2012

8 9 10 11 12 13 14 15 16 17

121817

# CONTENTS

# Chapter 1

## IS GOD A COSMIC KILLJOY?

As I travel around, one of the questions I am asked most often is "How can a Christian know the will of God for his or her life?" Most of us acknowledge that God has a plan for the life of every believer, but often we have trouble in finding just which way this plan goes at a particular juncture. There are plenty of books, pamphlets, and sermons addressing the problem, and yet the answers sometimes seem to elude even the most persistent searcher. My prayer is that this little book will help fill in some of the gaps in a fresh and practical way.

One may look for definite guidelines in this area but merely wind up with a variety of ideas. Some apparently think that God's will is lost. At least they say they are searching for it! To them, God must appear to be a sort of divine Easter bunny who has stashed His will, like eggs, somewhere out of sight and sent us running through life, trying to find it. And He is up there saying, "You're getting warmer!"

Others offer the suggestion that God's will is to be found via a dramatic experience. Running down the street, you fall on a banana peel and land on a map of India. Immediately you say to the Lord, "Thank You for that clear leading. I understand! India it is!" Or there is always the voice from heaven or the vision in your dreams calling you to Chile.

Then there are those who are actually afraid of the will of God. I will never forget the athlete who came up to me at Hume Lake Camp and said, "I'm not sure I want to give my life to Jesus Christ because

I am afraid of what He will make me do." He had the idea that God wants to take robust athletes, break both their legs, and make them play the flute. This implies that God is a kind of "cosmic killjoy," stomping on everyone's fun and raining on parades. People with this view actually fear the will of God as a severe way of life that will demand the sacrifice of their most treasured abilities or possessions.

Then there is the brass-ring mentality. Remember the old merry-go-rounds with the brass and iron rings? As the merry-go-round rotated, riders would reach for the rings that dangled from dispensers along the outside. If you grabbed the one brass ring among the numerous iron rings, you would win a prize. Some Christians see God's will like that: it's nice if you get the brass ring, but if you don't, just settle for an iron one. In other words, don't really run to win—just be in the race.

I have read in some sources that the will of God is nothing more than the "fortuitous conjunction of circumstances and impulses."

And so the theories go on and on.

In the middle of this muddle we still ask, "What is the will of God? Are there any concrete principles that may be simply stated and actually put into practice?" I believe there are! That is the point of this whole book. Can you know what job to seek, what school to attend, what girl or guy to love, what decision to make in any given situation?

Yes. You no longer have to worry. The struggle is almost over, the search almost done.

Let's begin with a simple assumption. Since God has a will for us, He must want us to know it. If so, then we could expect Him to communicate it to us in the most obvious way. And how would that be? Through the Bible, His revelation. Therefore, I believe that what anyone needs to know about the will of God is clearly revealed in the pages of His Word. God's will is, in fact, very explicit in Scripture.

As we look at some biblical principles in the following pages, be prepared for an unexpected and surprising conclusion that could change your life.

# Chapter 2

## THE CRUCIAL FIRST STEP

The will of God is no longer a problem for me—and it need not be one for you either. Let's start at the beginning and see what God has to reveal to us through His Word.

The apostle Peter highlighted the concept of the will of God for us in 2 Peter 3:9. Throughout his second epistle, Peter warned about false prophets, whom he called "springs without water" and "dogs returning to their vomit." Peter said that it is characteristic of these "springs" (which would seem to be sources of life-giving water but are not) or these "dogs" (who go back and lick up the vomit of their own once-forsaken sins) to deny two things. First, an apostate or false teacher denies the deity of Jesus Christ, denies "the Master who bought them" (2 Peter 2:1). The second thing that an apostate denies is the second coming of Christ (3:1–10). In mockery he says, "Where is the promise of His coming? All of you fanatics are running around saying that Jesus is coming. Where is He? I don't see Him." He reasons on this basis: "Since the fathers fell asleep, all things continue as they were from the beginning of the creation." He says, "Nothing will ever change, for it never has. I will never die. I never have. I couldn't possibly get cancer. I never had it before."

Peter would respond, "You forgot about the flood. All things haven't continued as they were." And they are not going to continue as they were! God is going to intervene in a great fiery judgment (2 Peter 3:10). "The Lord is not slow about His promise" (v. 9). In other words, just because we don't see God invading the world in judgment, it doesn't mean that

He can't. It doesn't mean that He made a promise and won't keep it. His delay doesn't mean that He is either impotent or unfaithful but that He is long-suffering, "not wishing for any to perish but for all to come to repentance" (v. 9).

This is the first thing about God's will: He wants people to be saved. So much so that He stays His judgment. Paul said, "This is good and acceptable in the sight of God our Savior, who desires all men to be saved and to come to the knowledge of the truth" (1 Tim. 2:3–4).

It is God's will that people be saved. If you are stumbling around in life and tossing up some periodic prayers to God but have never come on your knees to the foot of the cross and met Jesus Christ, then you are not even in the beginning of God's will. God has no reason to reveal to you anything particular about your life because you have not met qualification number one: salvation.

## God Leads His Own

A well-known New York restaurant and nightclub owner made this statement in a news interview: "I wouldn't be where I am today if it weren't for the Big Man upstairs."

Of course, that is a true statement when you consider what the apostle Paul meant when he told the pagan Athenians that it is "in Him we live and move and exist" (Acts 17:28). Christ is the sustainer of the entire universe, and nobody would be where he or she is today without Him.

But as to God personally leading those who have not received Jesus Christ as personal Savior, there is not a line of Scripture to indicate that this ordinarily happens.

Instead we read, "When [Christ] puts forth all his own, he goes ahead of them, and the sheep follow him because they know his voice" (John 10:4).

Without Christ, people are strangers to God. They are rebels against God, foreigners in God's universe.

The Bible says that God's will is that people be saved, and that is where it all starts. Jesus made this clear in Mark 3:31–35. He was already teaching inside a building when His brothers and mother arrived. The multitude was sitting on the inside, and it was so crowded that His family could not get to Him. Someone said to Him, "Your mother and Your brothers are outside looking for You."

He answered, "Who are My mother and My brothers?"

I am sure the crowd's reaction was something like, "What kind of question is this? Everybody knows His mother and brothers!"

If Jesus' first reaction did not shock them, His next words did. Looking about at those who were sitting around Him, He said, "Behold My mother and My brothers!"

Each person probably looked at the other and thought, *Who, me?*

Then He qualified it. "For whoever does the will of God ... is My brother and sister and mother."

What was Jesus saying? He was teaching that in order to be related to Him, one has to do the will of God. Turn it around. To do the will of God, one has to be related to Jesus.

The apostle John said, "Do not love the world nor the things in the world.... The world is passing away, and also its lusts; but the one who does the will of God lives forever" (1 John 2:15–17). Who is going to live forever? Those who do the will of God. But who is the only One who can give eternal life? Jesus Christ. The very first step in walking the pathway of God's will, then, is that you be saved.

If you have never committed your life to Jesus Christ, you cannot expect anything at all from God. He owes you nothing. He is not obligated to you in even the slightest sense.

People reject this. The doctrine of salvation is unpopular because it includes the recognition of sin. Nobody likes to admit sin. And many people resist the idea that they need to be saved.

## Confrontation at UCLA

I will never forget sharing in an evangelism blitz with Campus Crusade for Christ on the UCLA campus. About two thousand kids went person to person, sharing the gospel. At the time, UCLA was a stronghold of Judaism—Orthodox, Conservative, and Reformed. It was also known for its Communist groups. UCLA was thus not exactly the most open place to the gospel, but away we went, sharing Christ. Soon a front-page article appeared in the *Daily Bruin* with a cartoon showing a bruin (UCLA's bear mascot) lying on the ground with a Christian driving his heel into the bruin's neck. Included in the issue was an article written by the dean warning all those on campus talking about Jesus Christ to cease immediately or the administration would take "direct action." The dean cited an article of the university's constitution that said the "campus is not to be used for religious conversion."

Talking about sin and salvation is offensive to some people. Who wants to hear about sin? Most people mask it. Sin is not sin. Oh no. Sin is a "prenatal predilection," psychologists tell us. Sin is an "idiosyncrasy of individuality." Sin is "poor secretion of the endocrine glands"!

But God's will is that people be saved! And basic to salvation is the recognition of sin. This lays it right at your feet. Either you are not saved from your sin and you need to come to Christ because that is God's will, or you are saved and need to reach others with the message of salvation. There is a world out there that needs Jesus Christ. God wants them to be saved, and you and I are the vehicles for the transportation of the gospel. That is God's will.

You say you do not know what God's will is, but I'll tell you what it is. Above all it is that you know Christ and then that your neighbors hear about Christ. That is His will. So often we sit around twiddling our thumbs, dreaming about God's will in some distant future when we are not even willing to stand up on our own two feet, walk down the street, and do God's will right now.

God so desired that people be saved that He gave the One whom He loved most, His Son, and sent Him to die on a cross. That is the measure of His love, and that indicates how much He wills that people be saved!

# Chapter 3

## THE FIZZIES PRINCIPLE

As believers—people in God's family—if we do not know God's will, what are we? Uninformed? No. Searching? No. We are being *foolish*.

"That's pretty rough," you say. "The Bible doesn't talk like that."

Oh? Try this. "Do not be foolish, but understand what the will of the Lord is" (Eph. 5:17).

Furthermore, the preceding verse tells us we have to get on with it; we don't have much time. We are to be "making the most of [our] time, because the days are evil" (v. 16).

You say, "But I am looking for God's will. Maybe I am foolish, but can I help that?"

Yes, you can help it. Otherwise, the Bible would not command you to "not be foolish." The way to avoid being foolish is covered in the very next verse. "Do not get drunk with wine, for that is dissipation, but be filled with the Spirit" (v. 18).

First, if you want to know God's will, you must be saved. Second, you must be Spirit-filled. That is the teaching of the Word of God.

Many Christians say, "I don't understand why God hasn't revealed whom I am to marry." Others say, "Why doesn't He show me what job I should take, what business deal I should enter into, what I ought to purchase, whether I ought to move to another home, or what I ought to do about some specific problem? Why doesn't God do something for me and show me His will?" And all the time these people are not even Spirit-filled, which is clearly revealed as His will. Why should God show a person something if he or she is not even fulfilling that which God has already clearly stated as His will?

What does it mean to be Spirit-filled? Let me give you a short theology lesson. We will call it theology of the Spirit-filled life. When you were saved, the moment you received Jesus Christ, the Holy Spirit came to live within you. There is no Christian who does not possess the Holy Spirit. "If anyone does not have the Spirit of Christ, he does not belong to Him" (Rom. 8:9; see also 1 Cor. 6:19; 12:12–13). Yet it is amazing how many Christians think they do not have the Holy Spirit.

I have sat in church and heard sincere people pray, "Oh God, send Your Spirit," and I've thought, *No, He is here. He is here!* I have heard people pray, "God, give me more of Your Spirit," as if He comes in doses.

The Holy Spirit is a person; He lives within you. "Do you not know that your body is a temple of the Holy Spirit who is in you?" (1 Cor. 6:19). So many times we ask for what we already have! We pray for the Holy Spirit, and He is already here.

Have you ever analyzed your prayers?

You pray, "God, give me more love for so-and-so." The Bible says the "love of God has been poured out within our hearts" (Rom. 5:5).

You say, "God, I need more grace." God says that the grace He has already given you is sufficient (2 Cor. 12:9).

You cry, "Oh Lord, I need more strength." The Bible says you "can do all things" through Christ, who strengthens you (Phil. 4:13).

"Oh God, guide me," you say. *But He has already given you His all-sufficient Word to light your path* (Ps. 119:105).

## Complete in Him

When will Christians realize that they have everything? Peter wrote, "[God's] divine power has granted to us everything pertaining to life and godliness" (2 Peter 1:3). You do not lack anything! But so many emaciated Christians go around and say, "Well, I just don't have the power to do this or that."

The apostle Paul said to the Colossians, "In Him you have been made complete" (Col. 2:10). Complete!

What are you looking for? What are you asking for? James told you what to ask for—"wisdom" (James 1:5)—and that is the sense to know what you already have and not to ask for it! By the same token, we do not need to ask for the Spirit; He is in us already.

Since we have the Spirit, we also have power, as Jesus told the apostles: "But you will receive power when the Holy Spirit has come upon you" (Acts 1:8). The word for *power* in the Greek is *dunamis*, from which we got our word *dynamite*. It is a type of power that is massive and explosive.

You may say, "Oh yeah? I'm not sure; I think I'm a dud. I don't exhibit explosive power in my life; I don't even fizzle that loudly."

But the power is all there. What is so often not there is the release of that power. It is one thing to possess the Spirit; it is something else to be filled with the Spirit.

Fizzies are small tablets used to make soft drinks. They were wildly popular in the 1950s and 1960s, and they've recently tried to make a comeback. The tablets are basically like flavored Alka-Seltzers. Put one in a glass of water and its flavor is released. This concentrated, compact power pill is no good as long as it sits on the bottom of the glass. It has to release its energy to fill the glass, and then it turns the water into something new. If it is a grape Fizzie, you get a glass of grape drink. The flavor of the tablet determines the flavor of the water.

In a measure, that pictures how the Spirit of God operates in a human life. He is in the Christian all the time as a compact, concentrated, powerful, and personal force of divine energy. The question is, has He ever been able to release that power, to fill your life so that you can become what He is? A Christian not yielded to the Spirit does not manifest the Christ life. The Spirit of God has to permeate a life if that life is to radiate Him.

We cannot do anything apart from being filled with the Spirit.

I have a glove. If I say to the glove, "Play the piano," what does the glove do? Nothing. The glove cannot play the piano. But if I put my hand in the glove and play the piano, what happens? Music! If I put my hand in the glove, the glove moves. The glove does not get pious and say, "Oh hand, show me the way to go." It does not say anything; it just goes. Spirit-filled people do not mumble and stumble around trying to find out what God wants. They just go!

People often ask, "How do I know my spiritual gift?" The best way is to live a Spirit-filled life, see what God does through you, look back in retrospect, and say, "Oh, that's what I do when God has control of me. Apparently that is my gift." There is no need to get analytical. The whole point is that we need the Spirit of God to be released in our lives. This is simply a matter of decisions. When you get up in the morning, you decide what you are going to wear. Next, you decide what you are going to eat for breakfast. And so it goes through the day—one decision after another. The Spirit-filled life yields every decision to the control of the Spirit.

## Peter's Experience

An illustration comes from the life of the apostle Peter. When Peter was near Jesus Christ, he had amazing power. Thus he loved to be where Jesus was. On one occasion the disciples were out on the Sea of Galilee (Matt. 14:22–33). Their boat was tossing in a storm, and they couldn't get to Capernaum. (The winds very often turn the Sea of Galilee into a swirl, keeping a boat moving in a circle.)

Suddenly one of the men in the boat looked out and said, "Someone is walking on the water!" Sure enough, with robes flowing in the wind, here came Jesus, walking across the whitecaps.

Peter cried out, "Is that You, Lord?"

The Lord answered, "Yes, it is Me."

Peter said, "Can I come out to You?"

You may wonder why Peter said that. Why didn't he wait in the boat till Jesus got there? But that wouldn't have been like Peter. He said to himself, "Jesus is over there. I am over here. That is not good. I must go over there." It never entered his mind that normally he was not able to walk on water. That was not even a problem. When he saw Jesus, he had such a desire to be with Him that he went.

But when Peter got out on those tossing waves, he

looked down and thought, *What am I doing here?* He began to sink, but the Lord lifted him back up.

The point is that when he was near Jesus, Peter could do the miraculous. He and Jesus walked back together on the water.

Sometime later Jesus was talking to His disciples and asked, "Who do people say that I am?"

They answered, "Oh, some people think You are Jeremiah; some people think You are Elijah; some people think You are one of the prophets."

He said, "Who do you think I am?"

Peter responded, "You are the Christ, the Son of the living God" (Matt. 16:16). Then, I feel sure, he wondered, *Where did that come from?*

Jesus said, "Flesh and blood did not reveal this to you, Peter, but My Father who is in heaven did" (see Matt. 16:13–17).

Peter probably said, "I thought so. I surely didn't know that." You see, when Peter was near Jesus, he not only did the miraculous, but he also said the miraculous. Is it any wonder he wanted to be near Him?

When he was near Christ, Peter had miraculous courage. He was in the garden of Gethsemane when a whole band of soldiers—as many as five hundred—came to arrest Jesus. They came marching in with all their regalia. In front of them came the chief priests, and before the chief priests came the servants of the priests. Peter was standing with the Lord. Maybe his thoughts went something like this: *They think they are going to take Jesus away. No, they won't.*

Since Peter did not ever want to be removed from the presence of Jesus, he took out a sword. He started with the first guy in line, who happened to be Malchus, the servant of the high priest. The Bible says Peter cut off Malchus's ear, but if I know Peter, he was going for his whole head. Peter was ready to take on the whole Roman army. You see, when he was with Jesus, he had miraculous courage.

A little later Jesus went in to be tried, and Peter stood outside. He was removed from Jesus. What happened then to this powerful man—this man who could walk on water, speak with divine inspiration, exhibit miraculous courage? When he got separated from Jesus, he was a failure. On three occasions he denied Christ. Apart from Jesus, he was nothing.

## Ready for Burial?

But the day came when Jesus was to ascend into heaven. You say, "Oh no. If Peter is a coward when he is one hundred feet away from Jesus, what are we going to do with him when Jesus goes away into heaven? We might as well bury him. He's worthless!"

Yet, a short time after Christ's ascension, Peter stood before the enemies of Christ and said, "Men of Judea and all you who live in Jerusalem, let this be known to you and give heed to my words" (Acts 2:14). Wham! He took a text from Joel and away he went. He said they had killed the Prince of Life, desired a murderer to be released to them, and denied the Holy One. Then he proceeded to proclaim Christ fearlessly, firing the gospel out with both barrels. When did Peter get such courage?

The next time we read about Peter is in Acts 3. He and John went into the temple through the Gate Beautiful, where there was a man who had been lame for forty years. Peter said to him, "Look at us!" The man looked, and Peter said, "I do not possess silver and gold, but what I do have I give to you: In the name of Jesus Christ the Nazarene—walk!" (Acts 3:4–6). The lame man stood up and started leaping and jumping and praising God. Peter had not only said the miraculous, but he had done it too.

In the next chapter of Acts, Peter was persecuted. He exhibited a boldness that was remarkable, the same courage he displayed in the garden. You might say to yourself, "I don't understand this. Peter had these traits only when Jesus was near. Yet, with Jesus back in heaven, Peter displayed these same great traits again. What was going on?" Acts 2:4 gives us the secret. Before Peter ever did any exploits, he was one of those who "were … filled with the Holy Spirit" (Acts 2:4).

Let me draw a conclusion. When Peter was filled with the Holy Spirit, he had the same power as when he was standing next to Jesus Christ! Now there's something exciting! Do you know what the Spirit-filled life is? It is living every moment as though you are standing in the presence of Jesus Christ! Not too complicated, is it? Someone might think I am confusing the issue because the Holy Spirit and Christ are different. But by what name did Paul call the Holy Spirit? "The Spirit of Christ" (Rom. 8:9). Jesus said that when He went away, He would send *allos*, "another," Comforter (John 14:16 KJV). There are two words in the Greek for *another*: *heteros* and *allos*. *Heteros* means another of a different kind, but *allos* means another of exactly the same kind!

Here is my Bible. If I said to you, "Give me *heteros biblos*," you could give me any book. If I said to you, "Give me *allos biblos*," you would have to give me another Bible exactly like mine, with all my markings and cuts and cracks. This is *allos*. When Jesus said, "I am going to send you another Comforter," He said *allos*, another exactly like Me. The Spirit-filled life is nothing more than living in the conscious presence of the indwelling Christ.

We tend to get so fogged up about the Spirit-filled life. Paul said we are simply to be filled with the Spirit rather than being drunk. We are to be under the control of the Spirit rather than under the influence of wine (Eph. 5:18).

How does the Spirit-filled life express itself? "In psalms and hymns and spiritual songs, singing and making melody with your heart to the Lord; always giving thanks for all things in the name of our Lord Jesus Christ to God, even the Father" (Eph. 5:19–20). Then Paul went all the way down the line, describing the lifestyle of Spirit-filled people. Wives will submit, husbands will love their wives, fathers will not provoke their children to wrath, children will obey, servants will work well, and masters will be fair. This is how Spirit-filled people are to live (Eph. 5:22–6:9).

## Filled with the Word

The curious thing is that Colossians 3 has the same list: submission, speaking in psalms and spiritual songs, wives submitting, husbands loving, children obeying, parents not provoking, servants, masters. Only here Paul did not link such living to the filling of the Spirit. He said it is the result of letting "the word of Christ richly dwell within you, with all wisdom" (Col. 3:16).

Do you see what the Spirit-filled life is? It is being saturated with the things of Christ—with His Word, His person.

You might say, "Well, you know I'd like that. I'd like to be saturated with Christ. How do I do that?"

The only way is to study the Book that discloses all He is!

You say, "I tried reading the Bible, but I didn't get anything."

Let me share how I study the Bible and how the Bible has come alive to me. I began in 1 John. One day I sat down and read all five chapters straight through. It took me twenty minutes. Reading one book straight through was terrific. (The books of the Bible weren't written as an assortment of good little individual verses. They were written with flow and context.)

The next day, I sat down and read 1 John straight through again. The third day, I sat down and read 1 John straight through. The fourth day, straight through again. The fifth day, I sat down and read it again. I did this for thirty days. Do you know what happened at the end of the thirty days? I knew what was in 1 John.

Someone says to you, "Where in the Bible does it talk about confessing our sins?" You see a mental image of 1 John, first chapter, right-hand column, halfway down (depending on your Bible). Where does it say to love not the world? Second chapter, right-hand column, halfway down. Where does it talk about sin unto death? Chapter 5, last page. You know 1 John!

Next, I went to the gospel of John. I divided the gospel of John into three sections of seven chapters each. I read the first seven chapters for thirty days, the next seven for the next thirty days, and the last seven for thirty days. In ninety days I had read the entire gospel of John thirty times.

Where does it talk about the Good Shepherd? Chapter 10, right-hand column, starts in the middle, goes down, flip the page, go on down. Where does it talk about the vine and the branches? Chapter 15. Where does it talk about Jesus' friends? Chapter 15, over in the next column and a little farther down.

Where does it talk about Jesus' arrest in the garden? John 18. The restoration of Peter? John 21. The woman at the well? John 4. The Bread of Life? John 6. Nicodemus? John 3. The wedding at Cana? John 2.

You might say, "My, are you smart!" No, I am not smart. I read it thirty times. Even I can get it then! Isaiah said to learn "order on order, line on line … a little here, a little there" (Isa. 28:10–13). Then you have hidden it in your heart. After a while you are no longer concordance challenged!

## Planned Neglect

The more you study the Word of God, the more it saturates your mind and life. Someone is reported to have asked a concert violinist in New York's Carnegie Hall how she became so skilled. She said that it was by "planned neglect." She planned to neglect everything that was not related to her goal.

Some less important things in your life could stand some planned neglect so that you might give yourself to studying the Word of God. Do you know what would happen? The more you would study the

Word of God, the more your mind would be saturated with it. It will be no problem then for you to think of Christ. You won't be able to stop thinking of Him.

To be Spirit-filled is to live a Christ-conscious life, and there is no shortcut to that. You can't go and get yourself super-dedicated to live a Christ-conscious life. The only way you can be saturated with the thoughts of Christ is to saturate yourself with the Book that is all about Him. And this is God's will, that you not only be saved but that you also be filled with the Spirit.

# Chapter 4

## THE PRIORITY OF PURITY

To some people who have been looking for the will of God for a long time, this is going to seem quite obvious. "For this is the will of God, your sanctification" (1 Thess. 4:3). God desires every believer to be sanctified. What does *sanctified* mean? Let's use the word *pure* instead. In 1 Thessalonians 4:3–7, Paul talked about practical purity, and he gave four principles.

## Abstain from Fornication

Stay away from sexual sin. Paul did not say to avoid sex; he said to stay away from sexual sin. Of course, this means we must not get involved in sexual acts that are wrong. It also means we should stay far away from those things. Some Christians who wouldn't dream of doing those things sit and watch somebody else doing them or read about them in some book and call it entertainment. We should have no part in those things.

I am not a prude; I think sex is a glorious thing. God invented it. And because He invented it, it is good. But He designed it for the beauty of the marriage relationship and nowhere else. For people to think that they can cheat God and get kicks out of sex apart from marriage is to believe the devil's lie.

It is absurd for a young person (or anyone else) who is living in sexual impurity to say, "God, show me Your will." Such a person is not even doing what this text of Scripture says is His will. Why should God disclose some further will?

Stay away from immoral sex. That is a simple

principle. Someone inevitably says, "How far away?" Far away enough to be pure. Sanctified. Set apart wholly unto God.

Am I saying that you can't hold hands with the one you love? That is not the issue. Do I mean that you can't kiss? I don't mean that either. The Bible says, "All things are lawful for me, but not all things are profitable. All things are lawful for me, but I will not be mastered by anything" (1 Cor. 6:12). You can be blessed by God only so long as you are controlling what you do for His honor. When lust controls you, you have crossed the line. It's a simple principle.

## Control Your Body

The second principle concerning practical purity is expressed in 1 Thessalonians 4:4 (KJV): "Every one of you should know how to possess his vessel in sanctification and honour." In the Greek, there are two possible meanings of this word *vessel*: "wife" or "body." In the context, I take it to mean "body." Paul was saying that we are to control our bodies. That is purity.

We ought to keep our bodies in subjection to ensure that we are honoring God. That includes controlling the way we dress and the things we do with our bodies. This principle covers the whole area of the lust of the flesh, and not just sexual things. A person can dishonor God by overdressing to attract attention. Gluttony also puts a person in the position of dishonoring God and committing sin because it is obvious to everyone that the glutton cannot control the desire to eat. Nothing that gratifies the body to the dishonoring of God can have a place in the will of God.

## Subdue Your Passions

The Christian is not to live "in lustful passion, like the Gentiles [heathens] who do not know God" (1 Thess. 4:5). What was Paul saying? Don't act like the rest of the world—they are guided by their passions.

A young woman of sixteen came up to me one time with tears streaming down her cheeks. She said to me, "John, I can't take any more. I am going to kill myself." I asked her why, and she replied, "I have been involved with so many boys since I was thirteen years old that I can't look at myself in the mirror." We sat down and talked about God's love and complete forgiveness. That teenager invited Jesus into her life. Later her eyes sparkled through the tears as she said, "You know something? I feel forgiven." I assured her that she was. She went out from that place no longer to live in the gutter but to set her affections on things above.

One of the great, liberating things about Christianity is that it takes you out of the gutter and lifts you up. Stay up! Don't act like the godless.

## Treat Others Fairly

No one is to "go beyond and defraud his brother in any matter" (1 Thess. 4:6 KJV). In other words, don't take advantage of people.

Some people step on others' necks to get what they want. Some people use others in sexual ways to gratify their own desires. Others use people in business ways. There are many ways to use people. Don't do it, for "the Lord is the avenger of all such."

You may say, "I don't like those rules. God is narrow-minded." Then verse 8 is for you. "He who rejects this is not rejecting man but the God who gives His Holy Spirit to you." If you mistreat people, you really mistreat and despise God.

In verse 7, Paul summed up what we have been saying. "For God has not called us for the purpose of impurity, but in sanctification." God's calling—God's will—is that we be sanctified, holy, pure.

Robert Murray McCheyne spoke at the ordination of young Dan Edwards in the 1840s. He said something like this: "Mr. Edwards, do not forget the inner man, the heart. The cavalry officer knows that his life depends upon his saber, so he keeps it clean. Every stain he wipes off with the greatest care. Mr. Edwards, you are God's chosen instrument. According to your purity, so shall be your success. It is not great talent; it is not great ideas that God uses; it is great likeness to Jesus Christ. Mr. Edwards, a holy man is an awesome weapon in the hand of God" (see 2 Tim. 2:21). McCheyne was right, and God's will is that you be holy—sanctified.

# Chapter 5

## SILENCING THE CRITICS

Picture a young man who is very earnestly wanting to know God's will for his life's work. He's so dedicated to God that he's even willing to be a missionary, which seems to be the ultimate sacrifice in the eyes of some people.

But our young friend, despite his dedication, has some problems. He is a little headstrong. He seems to have trouble getting along with those in authority over him. His reasons for rebellion are good, of course, at least in his eyes.

Finally, our young seeker-after-God's-will takes his problem to a wise old pastor. "I believe God wants me to be a missionary," he says, "but I'm not sure whether He wants me to be a home missionary or a foreign missionary."

The pastor looks him straight in the eye. "Young man," he says, "what you need to be first of all is a 'sub-missionary.' You need to learn what submission means."

Hard words? Perhaps. But true. The apostle Peter wrote, "Submit yourselves for the Lord's sake to every human institution, whether to a king as the one in authority, or to governors as sent by him for the punishment of evildoers and the praise for those who do right. For such is the will of God" (1 Peter 2:13–15).

What is it God wills that you do? Submit. What kind of submission is He talking about? Scripture outlines several kinds, including to parents and other believers. But here Peter called specifically for the kind of submission that makes you the best possible citizen in the society in which you live.

Who is it that we are trying to reach? The world. If we are not the epitome of what a citizen should be in the world, we will certainly harm our testimonies. God not only commands our submission to those in authority, but He also clearly tells us the reason. "For such is the will of God that by doing right you may silence the ignorance of foolish men" (1 Peter 2:15).

Do you know what the critics of Christ look for in Christians? Faults. How are we going to prevent them from finding faults? Eliminate the faults. We need to put to silence the ignorance of foolish people.

How are you going to silence your critics? By living an exemplary life within society. That was Peter's point. The Christian is not a revolutionary. If there is a lawful way to make a needed change, the Christian takes that route. The Christian works. The Christian strives to be the best person he or she can be and to make the best contribution to society possible within the bounds of the law.

Don't ever abuse your freedom. Do not use your freedom as a cloak for being malicious and evil (1 Peter 2:16).

Someone will inevitably say, "I don't believe in this restriction. God has told me in my heart that it is wrong. So I am going to break this law or resist that rule."

Wait a minute! The Bible says not to hide your maliciousness under the blanket of so-called Christian liberty. God said, "Honor all people, love the brotherhood, fear God, honor the king" (1 Peter 2:17).

If you happen to be employed by somebody, be "subject to your masters with all fear" (2:18 KJV). You may say, "You don't understand my boss!" The Scripture continues, "… not only to the good and gentle, but also to the froward." The word *froward* means "difficult to deal with." Do you have a boss who is difficult to deal with? What are you supposed to do? Submit, lovingly and willfully.

## Shake the World

So many times I think to myself that if Christians ever learned to live the kind of life Peter described, we would turn the world upside down (Acts 17:6). But sometimes the world can't distinguish us from itself.

The apostle Paul called us who are Christians working for non-Christian employers to give them an honest day's work for a day's pay and show them that is the norm for a Christian (Eph. 6:5–8).

If you are the citizen of a certain state, obey the laws of that state so that people might know that your faith is real, that it reaches and influences every area of your life. I always get disturbed if a guy who has a Christian slogan on his car bumper weaves in and out of traffic like a maniac.

The principle of good citizenship is further upheld by Paul, who said that when the church chooses an elder, it is to pick one who is blameless (1 Tim. 3:10).

You may ask, "Am I supposed to obey every law in the land?" Yes, every law. If you do not agree with them, that doesn't change the matter. Obey them. Now if you know a way to work politically to change poor laws, fine; but until they have changed, obey them.

But what if they tell you to do something that violates God's clear revelation and command? Then do not obey them! That is the only exception. This is what happened when the Jewish rulers took Peter and John into custody. They told them not to preach anymore in the name of Jesus. But Peter and John answered, "You judge whether we ought to obey God or men." And they went right out of that place and started preaching (see Acts 4:18–20). The only time believers are ever to violate the law of the land is when the law either forbids them to do what they have been told to do by direct command from God or commands them to do what God forbids.

What am I saying? It is that God wants us to be the kind of citizens in the world who will draw the attention of the world. We need to be different. We need to have the qualities of salt and light (Matt. 5:13–16). That involves submission, which is clearly commanded in Scripture.

# Chapter 6

## FACING THE FLAK

Many would-be followers of Jesus come to Him with dreams of greatness, which are good in their place. Jesus put down the disciples for arguing about which of them would be greatest and told them that real greatness centers in being of service to others (Mark 9:33–35). But Jesus also encouraged their aspirations for greatness with such statements as "You who have followed Me … shall sit upon twelve thrones, judging the twelve tribes of Israel" (Matt. 19:28).

But in the will of God, greatness follows along behind suffering, often far behind. And if you sign on with Jesus with greatness in mind, you better be aware that suffering comes first. Otherwise, the will of God may begin to look pretty undesirable after you have been on the way a short time.

One man came to Jesus claiming he wanted to do the Lord's will. "I will follow You wherever You go," he declared.

Jesus replied, "The foxes have holes and the birds of the air have nests, but the Son of Man has nowhere to lay His head" (Luke 9:57–58). He wanted this would-be follower to know that the will of God involves suffering.

The apostle Peter wrote, "After you have suffered for a little while, the God of all grace, who called you to His eternal glory in Christ, will Himself perfect, confirm, strengthen and establish you" (1 Peter 5:10). Suffering is par for the course for Christians.

That is why the apostle Peter also wrote about "those also who suffer according to the will of God" (1 Peter 4:19).

Someone may say, "I should suffer? That part I am qualified for. Boy, do I suffer. I bear a real cross. My parents are my cross." Or, "My husband/wife is my cross." Or, "My mother-in-law is my cross."

But that is not the kind of suffering Peter was talking about. He wrote, "For it is better, if God should will it so, that you suffer for doing what is right than for doing what is wrong" (1 Peter 3:17). We are to suffer, not because we have failed to be the right kind of person when we were younger, not because we are antagonistic, grumpy, grouchy, or out of whack somewhere, but we should suffer for doing what is right.

When that happens, Peter said, "To the degree that you share the sufferings of Christ, keep on rejoicing" (1 Peter 4:13). You ought to be happy about it. "If you are reviled for the name of Christ, you are blessed, because the Spirit of glory and of God rests on you. Make sure that none of you suffers as a murderer, or thief, or evildoer, or a troublesome meddler" (1 Peter 4:14–15).

The passage continues, "But if anyone suffers as a Christian ..." (v. 16). Do you understand what Peter was talking about? Do you see what is par for the course? If you are a Christian who is living a godly life in an ungodly world, you will suffer.

The apostle Paul put it this way: "Indeed, all who desire to live godly in Christ Jesus will be persecuted" (2 Tim. 3:12).

You may say, "But I don't suffer any persecution." Then maybe you're not living a godly life in the face of the world. But if you do suffer, it is a wonderful thing. The Spirit of grace and glory rests on you (1 Peter 4:14).

Evangelism isn't just the preacher's job. It is yours. Nor is it completed simply by distributing tracts everywhere, however good that may be. Evangelism involves living a godly life in the face of an ungodly world. And that will bring persecution, because the world does not like Jesus.

## Out in the Bushes?

Consider the words of Paul as recorded in Philippians 1:29: "For to you it has been granted for Christ's sake, not only to believe in Him, but also to suffer for His sake." Here is something shocking. Suffering is linked with faith. The Bible never sees a Christian at any time who doesn't suffer—because anybody who lives a godly life in the world will get the flak that the world throws back. If you are waltzing through life comfortably, it either means that you are not living a godly life or you are living it out in the bushes in a place where the ungodly world cannot see you.

The Bible shows how we can live a godly life in an ungodly world with success. Acts 4 records how Peter once unloaded a bombshell sermon on the leaders of Israel. He blistered them so many times that I am surprised they did not stone him on the spot. When he finished preaching, the Bible says the Jews "laid hands" on Peter and John (v. 3). It was not to ordain them, we can be sure! It was to put them in custody. But the result of Peter's sermon was that many believed. The number of men converted came to five thousand. And there were probably another five thousand women and children. By the time the church was a few weeks old, they had won perhaps twenty thousand people. In the next chapter we hear about their multiplying, but it doesn't tell us how many because they were beyond counting!

But let's get back to Peter and John, who were thrown in jail for the night. In the morning they were taken out, and they were asked, "By what power, or in what name, have you done this?" (Acts 4:7).

I imagine Peter thought, *What a question! Does that guy know what he is saying? I get to answer that!*

In a way, Satan is foolish. He overreaches himself. He thought, *I'll fix them. I'll get them captured.* Do you know what happened? They were slapped in front of the Sanhedrin (the top leaders of Israel), and they preached Jesus to the Sanhedrin, an opportunity they never would have had unless Satan had arranged it. Satan does that all the time. He put Paul in the Philippian jail, and the jailer and his whole family were saved. He put Jesus on a cross, and what happened? Jesus redeemed the world. Satan doesn't really know what he's getting into. And God is sovereign.

Peter and John got into this thing, and they just took their suffering. They didn't hassle. There was no fighting, running, hiding behind a portico, or anything like that. They moved ahead in confidence that this was God's opportunity.

"Then Peter, filled with the Holy Spirit" (Acts 4:8), preached the name of Jesus Christ and closed with an invitation in classic evangelistic style. "And there is salvation in no one else; for there is no other name under heaven that has been given among men by which we must be saved" (v. 12).

## Not Out of Order

Picture Peter standing in the hall of hewn stone near the temple. The whole Sanhedrin was sitting there, including Caiaphas, who was positioned behind them in the high priest's chair. Peter was preaching Jesus! And he was not out of order. They had asked him by what name he had healed that lame man by the Gate Beautiful, and he was only answering them honestly.

Then the suffering got worse.

The authorities commanded Peter and John not to speak at all nor teach in the name of Jesus (Acts 4:18). Peter and John answered, "Whether it is right in the sight of God to give heed to you rather than to God, you be the judge" (v. 19). That was a question the Sanhedrin had a hard time answering because they fancied themselves religious and said they believed in God. If they said, "You ought to obey us instead of God," it would have plainly put them at odds with God. If they said, "You ought to obey God, not us," that would have also put them at odds with God and exonerated the disciples. Peter had stumped them.

The authorities gave Peter and John a lecture and further threatened them. They couldn't figure out any way to punish them because they were afraid of the people, so they let them go.

Peter and John ran back to the assembly of Christians, and they all had a glorious time praising

God. Then they prayed. They did not say, "God, protect us; they are after us."

They prayed, "Lord, take note of their threats, and grant that Your bond-servants may speak Your word with all confidence" (Acts 4:29).

They did not say, "Help us." They said, "Empower us and send us back again!"

"And when they had prayed, the place where they had gathered was shaken, and they were all filled with the Holy Spirit and began to speak the word of God with boldness" (v. 31).

What does the next verse say? "And the congregation of those who believed …" (v. 32). They had results! They went out and turned that town upside down.

It was a beautiful thing, you see, because they submitted themselves to suffering. They confronted their world boldly; they did not back down. They did not sneak out or get into "gospel blimp" tactics. They were not trying to slip the gospel into somebody's hip pocket. They confronted the world head-on with the claims of Christ, in love, and they let the chips fly. Do you know what happened? They got opportunities they never could have had otherwise, and God gave them more boldness than ever.

One of the problems of evangelism today is that Christians are not willing to stand nose to nose with the world and tell it like it is concerning Jesus Christ. The gospel is emasculated to accommodate everybody's prejudice. We need boldness. It is sad that the boldness of Peter and John is far from what most of us experience in our lives. I pray to God that He will give us more boldness.

## Confronting the Militants

On one occasion, I was invited to speak at a particular college, with fifteen to twenty thousand students, in Los Angeles. I was asked to speak on the philosophical basis for Christianity. Many people were there, including a radical, militantly anti-Christian faction of students. And they came to listen to what I had to say.

Sometimes when you preach, you just feel the power of God going through you. It is as though you are standing there but God is doing everything. God gave me clear thinking and a fluid voice. The auditorium was dead quiet, and I was ready for tomatoes and eggs. For one hour, I developed the philosophical basis for Christianity. The last ten minutes I spent proving that Jesus is the Messiah.

When I was done, the militant organization demanded that I be banned from the campus permanently. I began to get obscene letters in the mail and threats against my life and family. They also said they were going to blow up my church on some Sunday morning. I began to get vulgar and threatening telephone calls at two and three o'clock in the morning.

For the second time in my life I began to realize what it is to confront the world and to find the hostility that is meant for Jesus coming to me. I cannot say that I have ever had a more exhilarating or thrilling experience than in those days. (And they are still going on.) I confronted the world with boldness in the power of the Spirit of God, and things happened!

I could have stayed away from that campus that day for fear that it would wipe out my ministry or endanger my life. But I went. A student came up to me after the meeting, while we were still there and the rumbles were still going on, and said to me, "Could I come and talk with you?"

A week after our talk, he came to my office, sat down, and said, "What you said made sense, and I want to know Jesus Christ." He is a brother in Christ now, and his salvation was an outcome of my going into that inferno. And he has already reproduced himself by leading others to Christ.

You may say, "MacArthur, you didn't have to get yourself in hot water."

Oh yes, I did. I am expendable for the sake of one young man! If God wanted me even to lose my life, I should willingly lose it for His sake. That was Paul's attitude. Paul said that he gloried in infirmity, tribulation, necessity, even in persecution, because when he was persecuted, people got saved, and that is good.

A Christian is expendable. You may not get physical flak but may suffer intellectual persecution instead. You may be quietly ostracized from society. You may be politely shunned at the watercooler. People may take a "there goes the weirdo" attitude, which causes a deflated-ego problem. Every person wants so much to be accepted. But you cannot be accepted by the world and be effective for the Lord.

I am not a masochist. I take no pleasure in being abused, spiritually or otherwise, and I am not talking about going around saying, "Oh poor me. I am persecuted. Aren't I spiritual?" God help us, no. But I am talking about a willingness to be bold, a willingness to face the world and let the chips fly. Don't ever water down the gospel. If the truth offends, then let it offend. People have been living their whole lives in offense to God; let them be offended for a while.

Consider Paul's words in his letter to the Philippians: "But even if I am being poured out as a drink offering upon the sacrifice and service of your faith, I rejoice and share my joy with you all" (Phil. 2:17). What did Paul mean? If I have to die as a sacrifice for you to be saved, that is good. If I have to offer my life as a sacrifice for your joy, I love it.

In his letter to the Colossians, Paul rejoiced about his suffering. You may think Paul was out of his mind. But he wasn't. He said, "I rejoice in my sufferings for your sake, and in my flesh I do my share on behalf of His body, which is the church, in filling up what is lacking in Christ's afflictions" (Col. 1:24). What did he mean? The world would like to get at Jesus. They do not persecute Christians because they dislike them; they persecute Christians because they dislike Jesus. They can't get at Him because He is in heaven, so they get at you and me.

Paul said that he was enduring the suffering that was meant for Jesus; he was filling up in his body the afflictions of Jesus. The world is not done killing Jesus. Paul stood in the world's way so that he would get to die for the One who had died for him. In the same way, we should count it a joy to stand and take the arrows meant for Jesus.

Paul said, "I bear on my body the brand-marks of Jesus" (Gal. 6:17). These scars over here—these were not for me. They were for Jesus, but I took them for Him! Are you willing to suffer for Jesus, who suffered for you? Are you willing to confront the world? That is the will of God.

# Chapter 7

## YOU'RE IT

God's will is that you be saved, Spirit-filled, sancti-fied, submissive, and suffering. God's Word makes all this clear. Do not read on until you have grasped these five principles.

You say, "MacArthur, you were going to tell me what school I should go to. You were going to tell me God's will, specifically. You haven't done it!"

Okay, let me give you the final principle, but hold on to your seat! You may want to jump up and shout! If you are doing all five of the basic things, do you know what the next principle of God's will is? *Do whatever you want!* If those five elements of God's will are operating in your life, who is running your wants? God is! The psalmist said, "Delight yourself in the LORD; and He will give you the desires of your heart" (Ps. 37:4). God does not say He will fulfill all the desires there! If you are living a godly life, He will give you the right desires.

People say to me, "Why did you go into your present ministry when you had such an enjoyable ministry before in another area?"

I always answer, "Because I wanted to."

"Aha. Self-will."

I had a friend come to me and say, "John, I don't know where the Lord wants me to serve."

I said to him, "Marty, if you had your choice of any service in the world, what would you want?"

He said, "Oh, I have such a burden for my people Israel. I speak French fluently, and Paris is just loaded with Jewish people who don't know Jesus. I personally would like to go to Paris as a missionary to the Jews."

I checked him on the five spiritual principles and said, "Marty, have you done all these things?"

He replied, "Yes, I honestly believe that I am committed to Christ in these areas."

I said, "Marty, good-bye, have a nice trip."

He hesitated and said, "But I have to write to forty-two mission boards."

I said, "No! Go."

He said, "But it is only my desire."

"Then trust that it is God who planted it. Get out of here."

He joined a faith mission and signed up for France. We put up a big plaque in our church that read "Marty Wolfe goes to France." He raised all of his support, and today he is serving Christ—in Canada!

What happened? Once he was the right guy, it was no big problem where he went. He is in the city of Montreal, working with French-speaking Jews. He had the right idea; God had a different city.

This brings up another crucial principle. Imagine trying to steer and change the direction of a stationary tractor-truck. Tough assignment. It would take huge cranes and chains to even budge it. But once rolling, a truck weighing thirty-six thousand pounds is not difficult to control.

Once Marty was rolling, God took over the steering wheel with the strong arms of His will, and it was easy. I suppose God could have hauled in His celestial crane, picked up and pushed Marty in the right direction, but He likes to use people who are already moving.

Listen to this commentary on one of the greatest apostles: "Now as Peter was traveling through all those regions, he came down also to the saints who lived at Lydda. There he found a man named Aeneas, who had been bedridden eight years, for he was paralyzed. Peter said to him, 'Aeneas, Jesus Christ heals you; get up and make your bed.' Immediately he got up. And all who lived at Lydda and Sharon saw him, and they turned to the Lord" (Acts 9:32–35).

This thrilling account records that God used Peter to heal a sick man and start a revival. What a blessed experience of serving in the Lord's will! And neatly tucked into this event is a simple little thought: "As Peter was traveling through all those regions."

Peter was already on the move, available for open doors. That's when God directed him to Lydda. Remember, God has His richest ministries for His busiest saints.

We find in Genesis a fascinating illustration of the same truth: "He said, 'Blessed be the LORD, the God of my master Abraham, who has not forsaken His lovingkindness and His truth toward my master; as for me, the LORD has guided me in the way to the house of my master's brothers'" (Gen. 24:27). The servant was sent by Abraham to find a wife for Isaac. He didn't even know who or what he was looking for. But he was involved in service, and the Lord took it from there.

Get into the mainstream of what God is doing, and let Him lead you to that perfect will.

On his second missionary journey Paul fulfilled the ministry God had planned for Galatia, a large province in the Roman Empire. He successfully strengthened, encouraged, and confirmed the saints. The job, for the present, was done. But Paul was not done; he was moving. He was a pattern of persistence.

Paul headed west, not knowing God's will specifically, but rolling so God could steer him. The next province was Asia Minor with its cities of Ephesus, Smyrna, Philadelphia, Laodicea, Colossae, Sardis, Pergamos, and Thyatira. Paul moved with Silas and Timothy toward Asia Minor, thrilled with the prospect of bringing the gospel to the people there.

Suddenly, like a concrete wall on a highway, they were forbidden by the Holy Spirit to preach the gospel in Asia (Acts 16:6). We don't know how God stopped them, but He did. The closed door changed their direction, and they went north to Mysia, hoping to enter the province of Bithynia. But "the Spirit of Jesus did not permit them" (v. 7). Another roadblock. They had been stopped from going north and south and toward Galatia to the east. What now? At this point, we might have said, "All doors are closed; we may as well go home." But Paul didn't say that. There was still the west! So they followed the borderline between

Asia Minor and Bithynia leading west until they came
to the Aegean Sea. They were at the beach town of
Troas, and "a vision appeared to Paul in the night:
a man of Macedonia was standing and appealing to
him, and saying, 'Come over to Macedonia and help
us'" (v. 9). No longer would Christianity be thought
of as another Asian cult. It was going to Europe, a
whole different culture, a new world!

God wanted them in Macedonia all the time. But
He never told them till they had proved their faith
and persistence and couldn't take another step.

Keep moving—what a principle! So many people
sit around waiting for that celestial crane to move
them, saying, "I don't know what God wants me to
do." They need to start moving so God can steer them
to that area of service He has planned. Knowing God's
will may mean pushing down a narrow line until you
hit a dead end. At that point, God will open a door
so wide you won't be able to see around it—only
through it!

What was Paul's response? It is recorded in the book
of Acts: "When he had seen the vision, immediately we

sought to go into Macedonia, concluding that God had called us to preach the gospel to them" (Acts 16:10).

Paul responded immediately, and that is the only reaction when a persistent heart meets an open door.

I remember going to an amusement park when I was a boy and paying twenty-five cents to get lost in a maze. It was full of mirrors, open spaces, and clear glass. The idea was to find the open spaces and make your way out of the maze. One little kid gave up and stood in one spot, crying for his mother. Not I! I ran into glass and bumped into mirrors until I found the open spaces and emerged fifteen minutes later.

You may bounce off a lot of closed doors, but that is God's way of forcing you into His open one. Get rolling! Be persistent.

You see, the will of God is not primarily a place. The will of God is not, first of all, for you to go there or work here. The will of God concerns you as a person. If you are the right you, you can follow your desires and you will fulfill His will.

"Therefore I urge you, brethren, by the mercies of God, to present your bodies a living and holy sacrifice, acceptable to God, which is your spiritual service of worship. And do not be conformed to this world, but be transformed by the renewing of your mind, so that you may prove what the will of God is, that which is good and acceptable and perfect" (Rom. 12:1–2).

And whatever happens in your life, along the way give thanks, for "this is God's will for you in Christ Jesus" (1 Thess. 5:18). He's using the experiences in your life to shape you into His will.

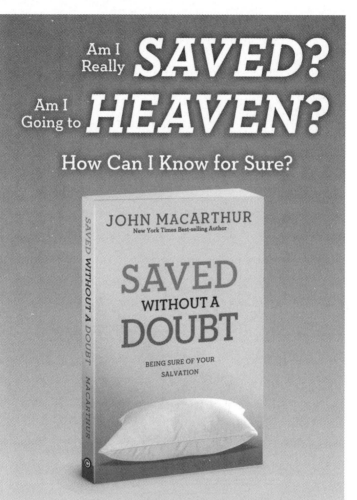